THE WELL OF LONGING

IRMA SHEPPARD

ISBN 978-0-692-45901-0 May 2015

The poems listed below first appeared in the following journals and online publications:

Beads on One String Heartland Pilgrimage 2013: "We Follow the Trail."
Heartbeat: "Unveiling the Burleson House."
Insights Community Newsletter: "You Alone Are Kissed."
OmPoint Circular: "Oh Meher, Compassion Is Your Name." "Someone To Carry the Fire," "Ghazal," "Trust over Hope."
Our Spirit, Our Reality: "Surviving Venice Beach."
SandScript: "first communion," "Surviving Venice Beach."
Where Love Could Take Me: "I wanted to be an archeologist when I was twelve," "No Resistance."

Acknowledgments

I am grateful to Mary Ber, Kathy Hill, Geneve Johnson, Ishwara Thomas and Jeanie Underwood for their support and careful attention to detail in many of these poems. I especially thank my husband, Karl Moeller, for his loving support, patience, skill and enthusiasm in effecting the publication of this book.

My deep appreciation and gratitude goes to Adele Wolkin, who shared with me intimate conversations she had with Meher Baba about Judas Iscariot.

Cover and book layout Karl Moeller

Satara well cover photo ©Karl Moeller

Avatar Meher Baba cover photo ©2015 Meher Nazar Publications, Ahmednagar. Used by permission.

All rights reserved ©Irma Sheppard 2015
Irma can be reached at ihs222@theriver.com

In eternal gratitude for the Presence of
Avatar Meher Baba in my life.

The Well of Longing

Emerged from Your nest of Oneness
I play shape-shifter: agate and iron
to mango, dragonfly and newt,
then cod and raven and elephant
and finally two-legged man and woman,
eternally God's fool on the brink of Now,
forever watered by the well of longing—
longing to shift beyond form.

Also by Irma Sheppard

Inheritance - 2013
Where Love Could Take Me - 2014

Edited and Co-authored by Irma Sheppard

Beads On One String Tour - 2010
Beads-on-One-String Heartland Pilgrimage 2013 - 2014

Table of Contents

Part One

Someone to Carry the Fire	7

Part Two

The Peace of the Place	15
God ForeverFar	16
first communion	17
White-gloved	18
Counting on Forgiveness	19
Receiving Your Silence	20
He Remembered Me Too: November, 1958	22
To Feel God's Presence	23
Idling in Existence	24
Surviving Venice Beach	25
Spring, 1980	26
Shining Out	27
I wanted to be an archeologist when I was twelve	28
Where Else to Go	29
Crossing Lines	30
This New Life	31
No Return	32
evolution	33
This Dance	34
This Day's Tapestry	35
Pilgrim, Hat in Hand	36
Darshan in Mandali Hall	37
Lodged in You	38

It Rains: Laurel Oak Cabin, Myrtle Beach	39
Oh Meher, Compassion is Your Name	41
The Kiss	42
Does It Please You?	43
Mehera's Beloved	44
You Alone Are KIssed	45
The Language I Dream In	47
Mehera	48
Epiphany	49
Handsome in Heart	49
I Belong to No Body	50
Ghazal	51
Beg for Obedience	52
Lament	52
A Lawless God	53
God Is always in the cards	54
Narrow Escape	55
Stepping Stones	56
This Fountain of Oneness	57

Part Three

Doves on all sides	61
Morning Walk	62
Unveiling the Burleson House	63
We follow The Trail	64
With Adele in the Original Kitchen	65
God knows He's not a he	66
Ajanta	67
Grace	68
Beloved	69
Execution: A Dream	70
In This Love: A Dream	71
Escape This !	72
Midnight Manna	73
Sun descending	74
Trust over Hope	75
This Path	76
In Venice	77
No Resistance	78
The Real Magic	79
Free as a Bird	80
Some Poems	80
Baba knows we're coming	81
My Heart	81
Love Runs through His Veins	81
Harvest	81
Om Point	82
Every time	82
Ocean	82
About the Author	85

Part One

Someone to Carry the Fire

Judas *

Yeshua challenges us:
Who is ready to declare his perfection within?
My every heartbeat beats toward Him,

but His eyes blaze so—I cannot meet them.
His hand on my arm, He draws me aside to hear
alone the mysteries of which He is Master.

Prophets must have kindled my infant fingertips,
for, despite dreams of the others stoning me, I burn
to please Him. *Judas,* His voice presses into me,

you will surpass them all—
you will hand over this form that clothes Me.
But you will grieve to your marrow.

Then, light-hearted, He points me
to a radiant veil in the heavens—
See, how your star outdistances the rest.

I taste the silence, the wild behind His eyes,
surrender to this blessedness—
I am taken up.

Yeshua **

Only Judas stepped forward
when I asked who among them
was capable of knowing Me,
and even he could not look
square into My eyes.

So I took him under a veil,
turned the key
and Myself acted
through him, had him speak
to the elders,

I who arranged
for the chief priests
to arrive at Gethsemane.
I who made him kiss
my cheek.

Dear beloved Judas,
the veil dissolved,
left then in horror
of what he'd been made to do.
It could not be helped.

Despite My own trials then,
I knew how the youngsters
tormented him, how he cast
the silver from his hand.
His every breath scorched,

he staggered as the wind howled
into his heart. Home nowhere,
he found his only refuge—
to swing
from a hollow branch

alone,
under the hissing stars—
this My mercy for his good service.
Afterward, his name a rose
upon My tongue,

I kept him with Me—
his everlasting Reward.
Someone had to carry the fire.

Judas' Niece   ***

I remember still the shame they flung at us
afterward, throwing stones at our house, slop
on our doorstep, calling us vermin to our faces.
On the second day, Father kept us from the well,
said we had to leave our lifelong home.

I think Mary really knew—she came, talked
in hushed tones with Father in the back room.
Afterward he said the Magdalene couldn't do much,
so opposed by the remaining eleven, jealous still
of secrets Yeshua had told her in close communion.

I was only seven then, Judas' favorite niece.
I remember how, the day before Passover, he came,
called me to his knee, his grave tone strange.
Always remember, he said to me, holding my face
between his hands, his eyes sober yet shining

in a way I'd never seen before—*always remember
to honor our beloved Yeshua, no matter what happens.*
His hands gave my shoulders a hard little shake.
Promise me! Something snaked in my belly,
but I whispered my promise.   The news

reached us some days later. Horror
shredded my heart—Yeshua crucified!
My uncle's betrayal! *It wasn't for the silver,*
Father told us. *He threw that away. One day
perhaps you'll understand—a hard task*

to prove his love. My dear uncle gone,
gone from me—they said he would rot in hell.
But Mary assured us, the night we left the village,
Do not despair. God loves our Judas and what he has done.
From village to farther village we fled, and again

the hot words followed us like evil bees. Even so
I felt the stern hand of Judas upon me, a command
to keep his secret. At last, a hamlet in the mountains
where Mother could keep her pots on the hearth.
Father took out parchments and ink, began to write.

I am eighty-one now, and all this I clearly remember.

---

* Based on information from The Gospel of Judas.
** Based on information received in conversation with Adele Wolkin, regarding her conversation with Meher Baba.
*** Based in part on The Gospel of Mary and my own creative inspiration.

PART TWO

The Peace of the Place

God was not welcome in our home when I was eight.
His place was in Sunday church—a mighty fortress.
But I never encountered Him there either,
nor His Son, Jesus, high above the altar, sunlit
brilliant in a red and blue stained glass circle,
kneeling in Gethsemane.

Jesus visited our Sunday School, called in by our hymns.
Jesus loves me, this I know, we sang.
I *really* wanted to believe that.
But He stayed safely closed in the Bible at our house,
where Mom was mean, Dad liked little girls
and my sister bossed me to bits.

I'd meet Him in the cemetery at the end of our block.
He stood there in statues, happy for sparrows and robins
to chirp on His outstretched arms.
Black squirrels chittered their way over grassy mounds.
A breeze danced through the high tops of oaks and maples.
He didn't say much, let me have the peace of the place.

God Forever Far

God seemed forever far away when I was thirteen.
In church, dressed in flowery hats, patent leather shoes
and white cotton gloves, I sang His name,
came away with *supposed to* and *shouldn't*
rather than *Jesus loves me*.

At home He was never mentioned,
never acknowledged
beyond the occasional *Gott sei dank!*

At night I knelt at my bedside, prayed
the Lord's Prayer in desperation.
Halfway through I'd think,
No, I have to really mean it,
so He can really hear it.

I'd start over, more slowly,
straining to mean each word.
By my third or fourth try,
the words still felt hollow
and God forever far.

first communion

I walk down the aisle back to my pew
the soft paste of the wafer still
stuck to my palate
the thimbleful of amber wine now
harsh in my throat

where are the transporting angels
where the promised light
the heavenly chords to sweep my homesick
heart full into the resonance
of God's wordless Word

His son's broken body
and blood
have been my yearlong silent quest—long
afternoons of listening to the pastor and now
not a trace of even the smallest grace

I am still fourteen
awkward
in a dress of white polished cotton
I weave unenlightened back to my wooden seat
to the uneven toll of a soundless bell

White-gloved

       my hands hold a black Bible—
I stand prim, perfectly posed before the altar
of Trinity Lutheran Church, confirmed now
in its Protestant tenets, wine and wafer as
body and blood of Christ, now salvaging
the cells of my being
       in this framed photograph
I am fourteen, frozen in a smile, a corsage
of pink carnations pinned on a dress made
for me from my design—high collar, three-
quarter sleeves, flared skirt—luminous
in white polished cotton
       I look chaste as a bride, framed
by a bannister separating me from the Lord's
inner sanctum, where tall candles glorify Him.
His cross crowns me—the secret promise
of transformation unkept—I feel unchanged,
grief rigid behind my eyes
       in this frame-frozen moment I face
the camera full front, but my feet already know,
know and are pointing me
       in a whole new direction

Counting on Forgiveness

On the verge of fifteen, after a cousin's wedding,
a dear aunt lends a book,
The Search for Bridey Murphy,

about a woman who, hypnotized,
the moon blazing through her eyes,
remembers a life before this one.
I read and my every hair rises to attention.

Every cell and fiber acts as if fences have fallen.
Electrified, my whole being vibrates
to a ringing, an awakening to some internal bell.
This life I lead has become too small.

Silent eddies—a mad blessedness—surround me.
Stones whirl and I cannot listen to the humdrum leaves.
I *know* this to be true, this life after life. Suddenly
I have a friend, this book, to walk with.

Will I just ask for it? Risks growl at me.
Smoldering woodchips curl red
into grey, become the ashes of a whisper.

I cannot give it up. I dare not ask, risk losing this book.
Aching for what is real, I let go— the keening of years
lost to darkness and my heart was shrouded in noise.

In the end, conscience curves and shunts.
I pocket the plum. I just take it.

Receiving Your Silence

You come to me in the night,
open the darkness of my heart,
touch where I have no skin,
kiss where I have no lips,

bliss me in spreading spirals,
have me to know
to know
I am not this body,

not this mind,
this finite, named person,
this fifteen-year-old girl—
I am that which is.

It seems as if You leave then,
leave me with bones again,
heart muscle to ache,
to long for Your return.

There is no one to talk to,
no one to tell.
And even You I don't know
well enough to call by name,

to summon to my need.
No.
Not for twenty-two years,
alone yet again, when You

in silence speak within me:
Meher I am.
That Which Is.
Closer to you than your own breath.

He Remembered Me Too: November, 1958
By remembering His lovers all over the world throughout that night, He was making an offering of His love to them. —- from <u>Lord Meher</u>

I didn't know Your Name
But You knew me,
thought of me in that night,
before I slept—
You came to me in such a way
I knew I was not I,
but something beyond
for which I had no Name.

To Feel God's Presence

I never felt God sitting with me in church—at eighteen I stopped looking for Him there—checked into philosophy and psychology at the university. His name mentioned, tossed about, scrutinized from many angles, but it was all head talktalktalk. No answers to my questions. I gave up on the Ten Commandments, threw out the Nicene Creed. Kept God and Jesus, needing them to know Something, needing Love to Be. Hung on to the Golden Rule to guide me for the Now. God and Jesus still felt untouchable and I knew no one in touch with them. I didn't always remember Whom I was seeking, so I turned to the arms of men. A husband, and when he left, a series of lovers, until I met one who seemed to know Something. Being with him turned me inside out and upside down, till I prayed from my heart—*Whoever You are, help me please.* This prepared me to feel God's Presence.

Idling in Existence

Give me a straw to hang on to
or two or three
not for my hands but
for my mind to play with
to measure, contemplate, addle and twist

A busy mind feels less
worries less

Give me back a straw to worry at
or two or three
anything so I don't have to face
what I face
when You take away my straws

When I have nothing
to measure, contemplate, addle or twist;
just me hanging in space,
idling in existence

Wanting to hear You
and still almost willing
to settle for straws

Surviving Venice Beach

Death at 45-D Ozone on the first day of spring—Donald's—after two years of running red lights at three a.m., rushing him to Emergency. Two years with four of us boxed into two small rooms half a block from the Pacific--one can't breathe, one has seizures, another has nosebleeds, and me—skullbones showing through in the mirror—wasted and wasting at thirty-six. Working with the mostly mad on Pico Blvd. and living in a fish bowl. Stale desperation inside. Outside—dog poop everywhere. Venice Beach—stepchild to its hallowed namesake. Sideshow to the City of the Angels. Sunday playdate for Hollywood stars. *April*, I lose my job—a blessing—collect unemployment. On the boardwalk I thread through crowds teeming with piano-playing, harmonica-playing, guitar-playing wannabes. Teeming with jugglers (a clock, a rubber chicken, a sandal), with Afro-beat drummers in dreadlocks, white girls dancing—long hair, long skirts, halter tops, bare feet. I walk alone, skirt past retirees hunched over canes. Dodge rollerskaters, boomboxes tight on their shoulders. *May*, a young black man, handsome, naked but for skates, up against a squad car, interlaces his fingers—his next stop—the nuthouse. *June*, I tag along with the Hari Krishna parade. Gurus ride on painted elephants. I take shortcuts through walkways of bougainvillea-walled beachhouses. *July*, I move to a secluded studio on La Paloma. Find God in the form of Meher Baba. Stop smoking Camels and dope, throw them into the dhuni, a sacred fire. One sun-struck August afternoon on the boardwalk, a long-haired dude quick-stepping behind me says, *Hey, you alone?* *No*, I say. *I'm together.*

Spring, 1980

I live alone in Venice Beach, California—
my children halfway across the country.

After two years of emphysema, the heart
of the man of my dreams gives out. He dies.

I am worn out, on partial disability, lose my job—
I can't really do it any more.

Yoga at five in the morning.
I injure my neck. Pain. I wear a collar.

I dream:

*An otter floats on its back in the ocean,
opening clams, rinsing and eating them.*

Awake,

I *know* I am the otter. Sustained.
Provided for. Safe. Content.

The man in the poster at the foot of my bed
smiles at me. *Don't worry,* He says. *Be happy.*

Shining Out

A bus stopped
just ahead of me
as I walked
down Main Street
in Venice Beach.
A man got off and said,
*I saw you from the bus and
I just had to come and tell you—
you are so beautiful.*
He gave his name, Paul,
and wanting nothing else,
left me standing,
stunned in the twilight.

When I was seven,
looking and looking
in the mirror for the beauty
I knew was in me,
I saw a pretty face, brown hair
pinned back with pink
cowboy hat barrettes.
I knew there was more—
but where?

That beauty was You, Meher,
hiding and biding within me at seven,
then somehow,
some glimmer of You, shining out
to startle Paul off the bus.

I wanted to be an archeologist when I was twelve

but now,
unlike some bit of winter blasting
down from Saskatoon,
I sweep gently at the dust covering
my true self,
blow lightly at family dirtstorms,
screen their troubling debris,
brush off their ancient insults,
tap tenderly at layers of ancestral beliefs,
peel away the stubborn layers of self-interest
plastered on my psyche,
and slowly, slowly
uncover the bonebits, the sinews and casings
that hold my heart secure
despite ravages of hoar and heat,
of loss, of hurt, of time.

Where Else to Go

Beams from Your face linger,
finger strings of my heartmind.
One hair from Your head
leaves me stranded
between worlds,
walking the blank.

The next step penetrates air
thinned by a paucity of substance
Knowing, not knowing—no
surety but to grasp the lack
of matter,
meeting the impact
of nothingness.

There is no return,
no comeback,
no sprightly saying
to say it all—
just one foot and the other
stepping forward—
now fine-tuned to spaces
empty and silent.

Sway this way,
You say,
the path is clear
despite stones and thorns—
this way leads Home.

Crossing Lines

Something
about You
invites me
to *dare*.

You look
directly
into my eyes
knowing me.

An aliveness
sparks
between us.

Like kids—
can you do this?
This?

I dare to
long for something
I have not been.

Dare to be
what
I do not
yet know.

This New Life

I break a glass jar, a nailfile.
Spill salad on the floor—
it's going to cost me something,
this new life heading my way,

this door I'm about to slip through.

It's already been settled—
Signed and agreed to
in my heart of hearts.

Now to just watch—
what torn away,
what unfolding?

No Return

Where is my threshold now,
what sill to step over,
jamb to pass through?

Veils shift in the stir of Your breath.

I begin to see past endless wants—
love of a man, silks and designer waters—
to the desire for Your smiling embrace,
the longing to please You.

The piercing of my heart.

At the mercy of such hospitality
I am home here now.

There is no *where* to return to.

evolution

the slow slide of snake
augurs the sporadic trail
of a lizard's tail

deep in the dust path
she is so out of being
who she once became

now a kindled soul
shedding skins of loveless life
shines as never before

This Dance

> "I will take You up now, Beloved, on that wonderful dance You promised."
> Hafiz rendered by Daniel Ladinsky

I know, Baba, I'm not ready
for that wonderful dance
You promised.
Just the next step,
just one more step toward
You who never disappoint me.

No routine with You—
the ultimate Bad Boy—
always fresh, this dance
newly scored,
choreographed
with me in mind.

O Wild Holy One!

This Day's Tapestry

A silver chain of sighs
echoes ache by ache

An angel comes to open
this mortal mother's heart

All summer I look to the east
longing for rain

Love drops moment by moment
into my heart

My heart soars into Your eyes
the welcome of Your smile

Words cannot keep up

Pilgrim, Hat in Hand

What do I know of praising You?
> I remember You upon waking,
> before going to sleep,
> at noon and other mealtimes,
> at the outset of a journey,
> a safe homecoming.
> I pray and sing,
> fold hands in reverence,
> tell others of Your love.

So what do I know of loving You?
> I obey, often—yet not perfectly.
> Greet someone lovingly,
> though do not entirely forget
> a long ago slight.

But what do I know of surrendering to You?
> I bow down, place forehead,
> even my heart
> on the foot of Your tomb,
> kiss the cool marble,
> the fragrant tuberoses.

> Your words resound
> within me at great loss
> as well as at victory.
> Even so,

What do I know of praising You?

Darshan in Mandali Hall

I fell at Your feet—
where Your feet used to rest,

I fell in fact
at the foot of Your chair,

Your intent, not mine—
I had meant merely to bow,

to place me seated
in attendance

at Your feet.

Lodged in You

I nudge stones to the side of the path
to make the way easier for the horses.

Their hooves and my feet grind
some minute part of the stones to dust.

Soil diminishes in my potted plants,
becomes roots, sprays of leaf and blossom.

I eat an apple, a fig, rice and beans—
they turn into muscle, energy and strength.

I say Your name
and it lodges in my heart.

I repeat Your name—
it dislodges mundane thought.

Each remembrance of You
releases some minute part of me.

I become a little more
lodged in You.

It Rains: Laurel Oak Cabin, Myrtle Beach

> *Those out in the open will experience the full Light (of the Avatar's manifestation), those holding umbrellas over their heads will receive less, and those who remain closeted in their houses will get even less—*
> *Meher Baba*

It rains
and Baba reminds me
I have brought
no umbrella.

Blessings pour down
and I have no protection
from His mercies
from His cleansing.

Raindrops like acid ants
swarm over my ego mess
eat at my longings
strip me of all cover
skin me to the marrow.

No, Baba reminds
me

I sit sheltered
and screened in
hear only the scatter of drops
the piddle off the eaves
the ocean's soft whoosh beyond the lagoon.

I am not yet naked
I am not yet drenched
not yet ablaze
not yet blown hollow.

It rains
and Meher promises
all
is to come.

Oh Meher, Compassion Is Your Name

When I cried to You: *help me help me,*
You answered from my deepest silence:

I am here. Don't worry. Be happy in my Love. I will help you.
Do your best. I will put everything you need right in front of you.

You answered my heart: *you are mine, forever.*
I wept hearing Your singular Voice, irrevocably claiming me.

But now, Baba, my ears ring from Your bottomless Silence,
While the world is crashing in on itself.

And all You want is for me to hold on,
Hold on to Your daaman.

Isn't it time yet for You to come to us on Your white horse?
Isn't it time yet for You to speak Your wordless Word?

Oh Irma, remember how He cushioned the soles of your feet,
Helped you up the stony hill on the palms of His hands?

Oh Baba, in the fullness of Your silent Love, I plant my feet
Like a child on my Father's, learning the first steps to Love's
waltz.

Oh Brothers and Sisters, whether we feel Him or not,
He walks with us. How could He not?

The Kiss

Hazrat Babajan unveils Meher Baba's Divinity - Pune, 1912

Here—
he comes again—
my boy—peerless.
Now.
I crook my finger.
He stops his cycle,
dismounts.
My boy—matchless.
Still I beckon.
He comes.
He comes to me.
My hands reach his face,
my lips his brow.
There.
It is done.
This kiss to awaken
Him
to all He is—
All He Is.

Does It Please You?

Does it please You when I bow to Your picture every morning around 5:22 and say *Jai Baba*, just after I've pulled on my soft cotton dress, just after I've splashed water on my mouth and eyes and dried them with my facecloth, just after I've flushed the toilet and put the lid down, after I've peed and maybe passed some gas, after I've bent my knees to sit, presenting my bare bottom to You—there, majestic and shining in the poster above the porcelain tank—after all that, Baba, does it please You—how I offer myself from behind, from on top, from in front and from inside?

Meher Baba smiles and says *yes* to me.

Mehera's Beloved

Mehera's Beloved is so fine;
I like Him so much
I say
Be mine, be mine.

He smiles
and says
Yes,
I will be yours,
all in good time.

In seven hundred years
Call Me,
Call Me.
Here is a dime.

You Alone Are Kissed

On the lips
on the nose
fingertips
between the toes
You alone are kissed.

On the forehead
between the eyes
on cheek or neck
between the sighs
You alone are kissed.

On the hair
on a shoulder
over the heart
growing bolder
You alone are kissed.

On the elbows
on the knees
anywhere
I darn well please
You alone are kissed.

Under the palms
on the street
in the doorway
how discreet
You alone are kissed.

Under an umbrella
in the rain
under an elm
in the lane
You alone are kissed.

In the morning
at high noon
in dusky evening
under crescent moon
Baba, You alone are kissed!

The Language I Dream In

I dream the sky is blueblack, heavy
with rainclouds, ominous and still.

I dream Karl hears Meher Baba approaching
the driveway and rushes out to sneak up on Him.

I dream Baba tiptoes past my window,
His hair braided back, tied with a pink bow.

I dream He tosses me a quick wink,
a forefinger to His lips.

I dream Baba, playing His usual game of hide
and seek, smiles at me as He tiptoes behind Karl.

What language is this I dream in—
all silence—not one word spoken.

I dream Mehera looks long at me
in tender recognition—opens to embrace me.

The sky is blueblack, heavy with blessings.
I dream of rain—not one word spoken.

Mehera

Unwilling
blossoms drop
from her hands,
one and one and one—
*what will I do without You
come back,* she cries
as they fall at Your feet.
Words drop from her lips,
*come back
how will I live without You?*
to mingle with the blossoms,
the tears dropped at Your feet.
Your form already laden
with prayer, garlands and tears,
it's her form,
hollowed by Your love,
she longs to drop,
to mingle her being
for eternity with Yours--
but now has only blossoms,
and the bloom of her heart,
to drop at Your feet,
and a very fine handkerchief
to place as a last kiss
on Your Beloved face.

Epiphany

Mehera loves Me as I ought to be loved,
Baba said,

dropping a clue
to the eternal Treasure Hunt.

Decades later, I understand—
she offers no No to His pleasure.

Suddenly
He's putting worlds into my mouth.

Handsome in Heart

Let me
see the world through
Your eyes of kindness.

Let me
not leave fallen fruit
to spoil in careless
despair.

Let me,
handsome in heart,
attend to the need,
leave love
in the air.

I Belong to No Body

Moment by moment
scenes fly by or crawl.

With love, I can do anything
without a wall of worry.

I am to bless each one
that comes my way—

sent for my good,
like these poems—

dry shells of my being,
skins shucked off, left behind.

The wind now
has its way with them.

I belong to no body.

Ghazal

Oh Meher, every moment wants and woes pursue me,
I worry day by day how, how to be free.

Even my wanting nothing keeps me bound—
in this everyday confusion I feel drowned.

How can I ever, ever reach that pure place
where nothing is between me and Your Face.

Oh Irma, come give your worry woes to Me,
let them drown in My Infinite Sea.

Just love Me, love Me and love Me—
your love for Me will set you free.

Want Me and your wants will fade
like the sun's beam demolishes shade.

Oh Baba lovers everywhere, listen to this—
His very Being invites us to Bliss.

Beg for obedience,

He says,
to open the shutters of your mind—open
them to the fields of knowing and not-knowing
that live beyond the ken of reason.
Ask Me, He says. I will help you.
But it is best to beg, to show humility.
Obedience is higher than love—no easy
thing to obey Me—it is My gift to you.
So beg—you have no idea.
Just beg.

Lament

Your name silent within me
dry as autumn leaves
blown to scatter and drift—
I long for the fullness
of Your gaze upon me
to warm my every part
and most especially my heart

A Lawless God

It's not simple to follow a lawless God.
It means you have to fathom your own tenets
And know that He, however, is ruled by none.
He calls it grace and tosses it around, so

It means you have to fathom your own tenets.
He offers guidelines, yet retires ancient sins.
He calls it grace and tosses it around, so
Everybody gets some sometime—grace and love.

He offers guidelines, yet retires ancient sins.
They are of the nothing, only love is real.
Everybody gets some sometime—grace and love.
True love is not for those who are faint of heart.

They are of the nothing, only love is real.
Those who don't have love catch it from those who do.
True love is not for those who are faint of heart.
Come sit at His feet. He will grind you to dust.

Those who don't have love catch it from those who do.
He breaks up your closed heart to awaken you.
Come sit at His feet. He will grind you to dust.
Give Him your imperfections, your broken laws.

He breaks up your closed heart to awaken you.
The heart is His temple, the seat of all rules.
Give Him your imperfections, your broken laws.
He'll dissolve them in the ocean of His love.

The heart is His temple, the seat of all rules,
And know that He, however, is ruled by none.
He'll dissolve them in the ocean of His love.
It's that simple to follow a lawless God.

God is always in the cards

no matter what hand I'm dealt.
Sometimes He hides
behind the Kings and Queens
or pretends to be an Ace,
a Jack of all trades
or a humble three of clubs.

Hearts are trump, He says
as He plays Himself without a sound
and wins my heart in every round.

Narrow Escape

Some say that Jesus played dead
to put us off His trail, and
after tipping His hand
of having survived the cross,
letting His disciples know
all was not lost, and
after recuperating from
wounds of spikes and sword,
He skipped town with Bartholomew
leaving sorrowing crowds, and
headed east to share His Love
with the lost tribes of Israel, and
on to India, to continue His
Universal Work.

This feat was no magic,
but a higher order of law —
samadhi, it's called in Sanskrit,
a state of oneness with God,
while the body looks dead,
forgotten.

Convenient? Sly? Godly attributes?
But don't we already know
God is ruthless and relentless —
He will have His way, and we,
after countless narrow escapes,
sooner or later come around
to loving Him.

Stepping Stones

Dreams at three and four, warning me away from my family,
and
certain at fourteen that with first communion I'd be altered,
but
profound disappointment
until
at fifteen, moments of sweet Oneness
which
led me to know I am not this body, this Irma,
that
I too am That Which Is—but I could not abide there long,
and
knowing no one who understood, I remained silent,
until
I told Donald on a bench in Piraeus—he seemed to know,
and
led me to Meher Baba: *He says He is God*. I wondered—
then
Kathy offered the poster, *Don't Worry, Be Happy*
and
the book, *Listen Humanity*, edited by Don Stevens—I read
and
it answered all my questions, and ones I didn't know I'd had,
then
one day His Presence came to me, came through me—

now
I know He is Who He says He is—
then
all the losses of family, home, health, and work made sense,
and
all posed as stepping stones from turbulence
toward
ever still waters.

This Fountain of Oneness

There is only one dying—
to leave off what I want.

How to live then?

Give Me everything, He says,
and I will give you Nothing.

Part Three

Doves on all sides

in the rafters of the portico, in the grapefruit and orange trees, strutting around the pool, hopping onto the blue float to dip down for cool sips. The coo of the mourning doves is drowned out by white-winged doves, who spend hours calling, *Who cooks for you? Who cooks for you?* Thirty-three years ago I sat in the women's garden at the Meher Pilgrim Center in Meherabad, India. Bougainvillea brilliant in every corner. Sunny, quiet afternoons sprinkled with dove calls. The peace of the place took hold of me. *Please Baba*, I begged, *I don't want to go back to a big city. No more Detroit, no more Los Angeles.* One last summer in Detroit followed—just long enough to meet and get to know Karl. A year in Norfolk—a beach house hard by Chesapeake Bay. With Karl now in Tucson. And doves cooing on all sides bring me full circle.

Morning Walk

My shadow stretches out before me,
confident, grander than life.
I want it to walk beside me—
no room, it says, the path is too narrow.
It's true—prickly pear, barrel cactus, cholla
loom from each side of the stony way.
I clamber down, watch out
for loose rocks and snakes.
My shadow lengthens,
joggles around, seems to laugh
as if leading me along, showing the way.
It longs for tea with cream,
slender hips, wash and wear hair,
pelicans skirting the seashore,
breathing easy under fluorescent skies.
This is the life, it says.
I lean in to hear better.
Suddenly
feel a stone in my shoe,
a thorn in my sock.
By the time I've emptied my shoe,
my shadow, less jaunty,
has emptied itself, curling
up into me as if for refuge,
as if for dreamless sleep,
leaving me awakened.

A cardinal flames before me.

Unveiling the Burleson House

We enter, examine the house room by room,
hall, closet and cellar, upstairs
and down, as if it were a newborn—
in wonder and delight we discover
the grace in each fingernail and toe.

Baba is our constant Companion
in the eye of each smile,
the sweetness of our greetings,
in the rose on the teacup,
the heart of every song.

His all-seeing eyes follow us
from His photographs on the walls.
He blesses our pilgrimage,
our tea and cookies, songs and stories,
our quiet sitting, the humming in our veins.

Under His gracious gaze we meet long lost kin.
All my relations, we say.
All my children, He says.
How happy I am you are here, He says.
How happy we are that You are here, we say.

Here, we are the American Dream Family
gathered whole again, indivisible
in the American Dream Home—
Meher Baba dreaming us
into the Reality of His Love.

We follow The Trail

hallowed by tears and blood
of those true to One Heart,
hallowed by the Creator's own Footprint.

We ride and we tread lightly,
to not erase the power and the sorrow
of their plight, but to harmonize
those efforts, those losses,
with forgiveness
in order to realize God's True Intent.

With eyes of kindness for all,
we offer ourselves utterly
in Beloved God's service.

Written for the 2013 Beads-on-One-String Heartland Pilgrimage.

With Adele in the Original Kitchen

She holds my hand as I sit on her left,
looks at me again with eyes knowing and kind.

What shall we talk about, she asks,
knowing as I do that it matters not.

Nor the roomful of others around us
as I sit full quiet on her left.

Heart and eyes smiling of that fullness,
as if it were He I sit next to, on His left.

His eyes upon me, eyes of kindness—
This moment mine to keep.

God knows He's not a he

It's just that when He comes to Earth,
into the world of illusion, the realm of polarity,
He chooses to choose, not because He must,
but because He doesn't want to confuse us.
We have such a hard time recognizing Him.

He chooses a form at least half of us can relate to.
Formless as He really is,
He takes on a moustache-beard gender,
so we see Him as Father, Son, Brother, Friend—
male, in this past Cycle of cycles.

In my secret heart I wonder if He came to us
as female in cycles of long before.
Then God was full-breasted—
Mother, Daughter, Sister, Friend—
still the same Being.

Ajanta

From top down they carved deep into soft rock—
caves to line the length of the curved valley.
From top down they chiseled
Buddha's top knot,
the snails still warming his head,
down to his beneficent smile, elongated earlobes.
In each cave a Buddha in the rear chamber,
fingers poised in mudra.
The antechamber
graced with pillars, fluted or ringed with
lotus, from the top down to the leveled stone floor.
Walls lined with Buddha's life in bas-relief
and now peeling frescos.
Porticos and steps
carved up and down link cave to cave.
Windows fashioned in stone—views of where
we've been, where headed.
Sudden doorways
open to green valley far below.
From the top down they sculpted the ankles, heels,
each toe and nail of the Buddha's blessed
feet from which arose
rapturous scents,
celestial tones, reverberating
ecstatic throughout every chamber,
beyond all time,
all place.

Grace

Everyone recognizes Grace
not perhaps for what it Is
but for what each longs for

and like the five blind men
encountering
their first elephant

one perceives the ease of speech
another the beauty
the charisma

the poise of fitting in
anywhere, with anyone,
the mogul, the sweeper

insider or outcast
everyone recognizes Grace
and longs for

even the smallest part.

Beloved

I wish one day to see
my Self
deep deep within
Your eyes

me this piece of You,
as if You could
really be divided—
that's the joke,
isn't it?
In this crazy-quilt world
it's all You masquerading
as me.

Execution: A Dream

My daughter and I are caught.
She sits upright beside me. I do not look at her.
They are going to shoot us.
We have not done anything wrong.
But they have the guns, they have the power.
We look straight ahead.
They talk and move around behind us.
I hear the shot, feel her slump.
She is gone. I'm next.
I think about the impact of a bullet entering me,
and wonder that I am not afraid.
Without forethought I say,
Meher Baba, Meher Baba, Meher Baba.
I sense the revolver, cold, at the back of my neck.

I waken,
feel myself rushing back into my body.

In This Love: A Dream

A young man, dark-haired,
takes me to dance.
I have long awaited him.
I step into his arms.
Something fixes my eyes
onto his sandaled feet.
I exist solely to move
in utter harmony
with his steps.
We dance to music within.
I gaze into his dark timeless eyes—
there is no stopping —
lose and gain myself in their depth.
I *know* he is the One.
I am whole in this Love.

Escape This!

> *There is a slave loose not far from us.*
> *He escaped today from a cruel master.*
> —*Hafiz rendered by Daniel Ladinsky*

Desire moves me
sometimes forward
sometimes back
with my eye
on some thing
I think I lack.

A car, a house,
a friend, a view,
a ride, a trip,
a blouse, a shoe,
a flower, a stream,
a love that's true.

Heart blind and blunted,
desire moves me
to move much faster,
pursue that something
I'm so madly after,
desire—the cruelest master.

Midnight Manna

Why wish on falling stars—
meteors streaking across midnight skies.
Why pin hopes on burning rock
hurtling through a barren atmosphere.

Let hopes burn in radiant flashes.
Let wishes flame to powdery ash.

Stake all on the unwavering depth
of Love in His eye.

Sun descending

to the western horizon,
a brilliant white
saturates the room,
lampshade profile
sharpens on the wall,
spider plant leaves
spray graceful shadows,
a stark silhouette
stalks a carved coyote.

Sun embraces the horizon,
light softens to cream,
shadows mellow,
cream thickens to buttercup,
gleams amber, ripens to apricot,
deepens to fierce marigold.
Outlines seep slowly
into the light,
afterglow pales and fades.

Within me, a great need for emptiness.

Trust over Hope

Senseless,
trust comes from nothing
seen, heard, smelled, tasted, touched,
nothing read, said or thought.

Trust—
better than one-pointed hope,
which stems from the ever present I—
I—capitalized but false nonetheless.

Trust—
a gift, a grace,
reaching far
into Your immeasurable scope.

This Path

I walk this path,
stony or sandy in turn,
choose right or left by whim—
a desire for sun or shade,
for shorter or longer route this time,
as in rounds of lifetimes—

the push of birth, a first tooth,
learning to tie shoelaces,
my own driver's license at last,
a job, a child, a mortgage,
the ache of greying joints—

and the moment of return,
that need for a great emptiness—

again I set out--
this curve,
this clump of cactus,
birdsong, packrat nest,
shade of mesquite,
fragrance of desert rain,

this steep slope
and slippery descent.

This path—always narrow,
still littered with what came before,
even my own footprints.

In Venice

it was that first walk from the canal to the monastery
dragging my suitcase through a foot of fallen leaves
walking a long block under an arcade
of hugely tall trees, dry leaves clumping
under the wheels of my American Tourister
a slight breeze soughing above in the afternoon shade—
this short walk welcoming me to a city
otherwise entombed in stone

No Resistance

Love like water
flows
into spaces of least resistance.

God as Love
resides
in places of least resistance.

When I least resist
God,
I am deeply fulfilled.

When I have no resistance
to Love,
I will be one with God.

The Real Magic

A magic show is all tricks—
sleight of hand,
the hand quicker than the eye,
multi-colored scarves, rabbits,
hats and false bottoms.

But magic comes from the Magi,
the knowers of All,
who can manipulate the seen
and the unseen—water to wine,
fishes, loaves, raise the dead,
walk on water.

To them, these are tricks as well,
to bend our disbelief
into believing what we cannot see.
The real trick, they say, is to melt
a heart of steel into gold,
to sling a silver tongue
into silence and longing.

For this they summon
their most potent weapon
to banish all demons,
slay fiery dragons and
vanquish all doubt,
the only *real* magic—

the power of Love.

Free as a bird

we say.
Yet birds are not so free,
but confined to feathers,
to the patterns they fly.
Solo or in formation,
they are placed into their
particular bird space.

Some Poems

like so many empty boxes
after the Christmas tree spree,
litter my books.

A few still hold heat,
something given and taken
heart to heart.

Baba knows we're coming

she says, like it means
something singular—something
silken in store for us.

My Heart

longs to be brilliant
like a diamond in the eye,
but softer

Love Runs through His Veins

Love runs through His veins
while we nurse our hurts and sighs
Love runs through His veins.

Harvest

We're all in Baba's feedlot—
He's fattening us up
growing our plummy egos
so He can pluck them off
when they're ripe
and no longer rotten.

Om Point

There is no end
Can the beginning
be far behind?

Every time

I think perhaps I'm done with this life's deeds,
ready, perhaps, to leave this form,
I see suddenly a window
where there was none before,
and then a door,
which I'm suddenly through
and into the next vast adventure—
yet still
still in Your arms

Ocean

Sometimes
      this thunderous Lover sprays me with foam.
Sometimes
      this mellifluous Friend murmurs, *come home,*
                                          come home.

About the Author:

Irma Sheppard was born Irmhild Hexel in Germany in 1943. Her family emigrated to Canada in 1948 and to the United States in 1962. She has lived in Michigan, California, Virginia, and for the past thirty-some years with her husband and a succession of cats in Tucson, Arizona, where she is in private practice as a psychotherapist. Her short story, "The Human Touch: A Triptych"  won the Martindale Literary Award in 2000, and was published in *Kaleidoscope*, an anthology of Martindale winners. Her short story, "A Real Piece of India" was published in *SandScript* and in *Portrait*. She edited and co-authored *Beads On One String Tour 2010* and *Beads-on-One-String Heartland Pilgrimage 2013*. Her first book of poems, *Inheritance,* came out in 2013. Her second book, poetry and prose, *Where Love Could Take Me* was published in 2014.

After reading *Listen Humanity*, by Meher Baba, edited by Don Stevens in 1980, she received the conviction that Meher Baba was Who He said He was, and is—the Avatar of this Age—God in human form. This experience continues to shape her life.

She can be reached at ihs222@theriver.com

www.ingramcontent.com/pod-product-compliance
Lightning Source LLC
Chambersburg PA
CBHW072102290426
44110CB00014B/1797